MEET THE GREATS

Michelle
OBAMA

TIM COOKE

Gareth Stevens
PUBLISHING

Please visit our website, www.garethstevens.com.
For a free color catalog of all our high-quality books,
call toll free 1-800-542-2595 or fax 1-877-542-2596.

Cataloging-in-Publication Data

Names: Cooke, Tim.
Title: Michelle Obama / Tim Cooke.
Description: New York : Gareth Stevens Publishing, 2020. | Series: Meet the greats | Includes glossary and index.
Identifiers: ISBN 9781538252468 (pbk.) | ISBN 9781538252475 (library bound)
Subjects: LCSH: Obama, Michelle, 1964---Juvenile literature. | Presidents' spouses--United States--Biography--Juvenile literature. | Legislators' spouses--United States--Biography--Juvenile literature. | African American women lawyers--Illinois--Chicago--Biography--Juvenile literature.
Classification: LCC E909.O24 C66 2020 | DDC 973.932092 B--dc23

Published in 2020 by
Gareth Stevens Publishing
111 East 14th Street, Suite 349
New York, NY 10003

Copyright © 2020 Brown Bear Ltd

Picture credits: Front cover: Character artwork Supriya Sahai. Interior: Alamy: INTERFOTO 31; AP: Ron Edmonds 30; iStock: marchello74 21; Library of Congress: 11tl, 11br Jack Delano 15b; NARA: 35t; Obama for America: 23; Public Domain: Firstcultural 8, John Phelan 12 Antonio Vernon 9; Shutterstock: S Bakley, 19, Lester Balagadia 18, Pamela Brick 20, David Byron 15t Curioso 24, Everett Collection 33, Everett Historical 14, FeyginFoto 22, Frontpage, 34, Nicholas Glass 35b, Alexandros Michailidis 43, Page Light Studios 25t, Paul Brady Photography 28, EQ Roy 13, Henryk Sadura 25b, Joseph Sohm 32, 42, Tupungato 10; U.S. Federal Govenrment; Samantha Appleton/White House Photo 38, Chuck Kennedy/White House Photo 40, Pete Souza/White House Photo 41, U.S. Senate 20.

Character artworks © Supriya Sahai
All other artworks © Brown Bear Books Ltd

All rights reserved. No part of this book may be reproduced in any form without permission from the publisher, except by a reviewer.

Printed in the United States of America

CPSIA compliance information: Batch #CW20GS: For further information contact Gareth Stevens,
New York, New York at 1-800-542-2595.

Contents

Introduction 4
Chicago Upbringing 6
   Feature: Slavery 14
Law and Civic Duty 16
   Feature: Social Activism 24
A Political Wife 26
   Feature: The First Lady 34
The White House and After 36
Timeline 44
Glossary 46
Further Resources 47
Index 48

Introduction

Growing up in Chicago, Michelle Obama never imagined that she would become the first African American First Lady.

Michelle was brought up in a one-bedroom apartment. Her great-great-grandfather had been a slave. Michelle was smart and worked hard. She went to a good high school and then studied at Harvard Law School. She was working as a lawyer when she met her future husband, Barack Obama.

As a young woman, Michelle had dreams and ambitions: to help people and to fulfill her potential. Inspired by her parents, she was determined to make the most of every opportunity. She did this even when it seemed there were many obstacles in her way: because of her skin color and because she was a woman. She had many achievements, first as a successful lawyer and then as a remarkable First Lady. After she left the White House in 2017, she continued to be a passionate supporter of empowerment for girls around the world.

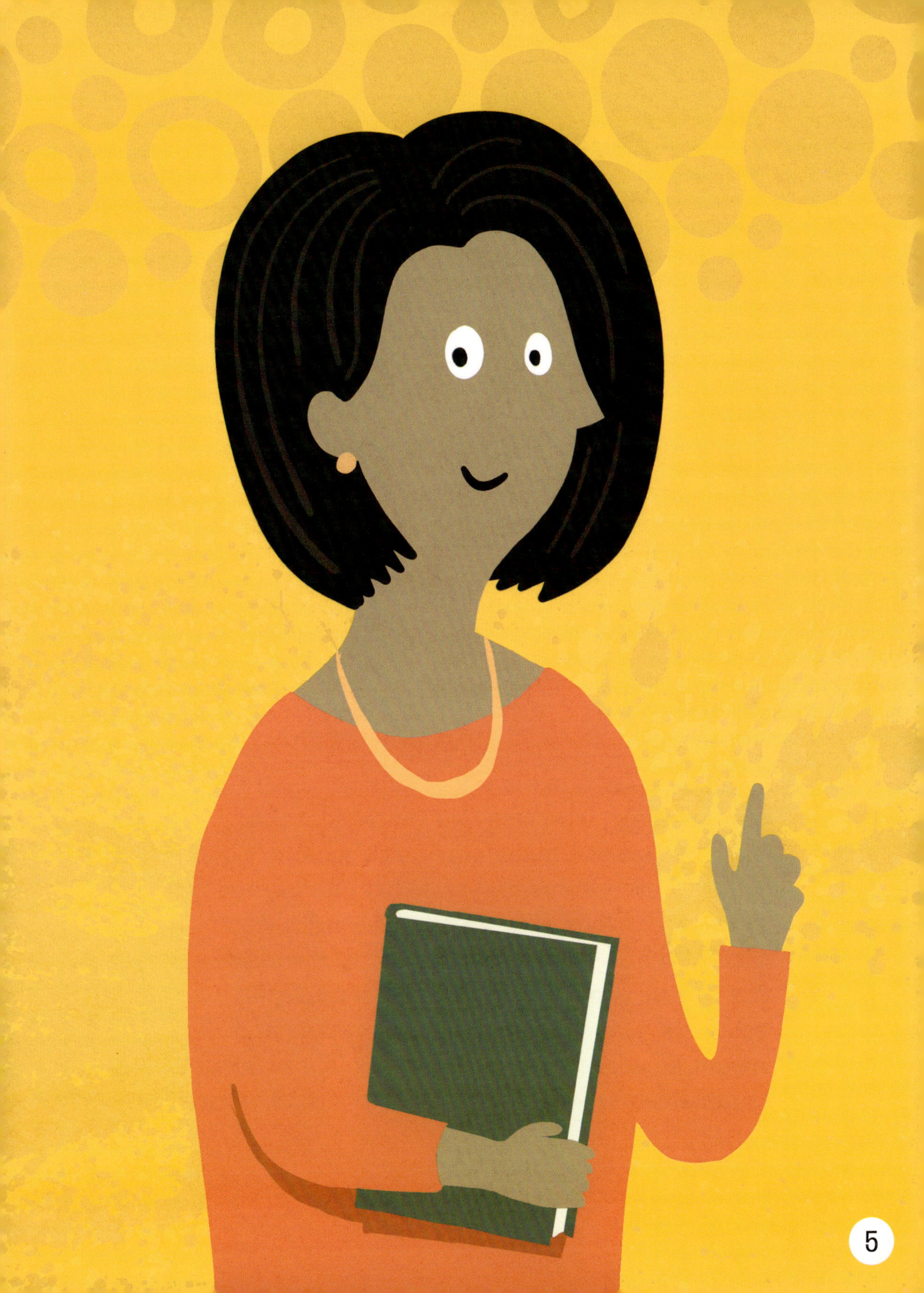

Chicago
UPBRINGING

A descendant of slaves, Michelle LaVaughn Robinson would graduate from one of the best law schools in the country, Harvard Law School.

Michelle was born January 17, 1964, on Chicago's South Side. Home was a one-bedroom apartment where she lived with her mom, Marian, and her dad, Fraser, and her brother Craig, who was two years older than Michelle. Marian had worked as a secretary but quit to stay at home and raise her children. Fraser worked as a manager at the city's water plant. He had started as a janitor and worked his way up despite being sick with **multiple sclerosis**. The disease affected his spine and meant he needed crutches to walk, but he never complained and he never called in sick to work.

MEET THE GREATS: MICHELLE OBAMA

QUICK FACTS

- Michelle grew up on the South Side of Chicago.
- She and her brother were both hardworking students who went to one of Chicago's best high schools and to Princeton University.

A HAPPY HOME

The family did not have much money, but Michelle's parents raised their children to work hard, help people, and get the best education possible. Craig was not only a straight-A student, but he was also a talented basketball player. He was a hard act for Michelle to follow, but she was very competitive. The family played board games in the evenings and Michelle always wanted to win.

Michelle grew up on the South Side of Chicago.

At Bryn Mawr Public Elementary School, Michelle skipped second grade, just as her brother had done. Like her brother, she was a straight-A student. In sixth grade, she was chosen for a gifted student program. Instead of attending the local high school, in 1977 she went off to Chicago's first **magnet school**.

HIGH SCHOOL

The Whitney M. Young Magnet High School was named for a **civil rights** campaigner. It was for the highest-achieving students in Chicago. However, the school was 12 miles (18 km) from the Robinsons' home. For four years, Michelle had to do a two-bus 90-minute **commute** to and from school. Whitney Young was a very **progressive** school. It aimed for a 50–50 split between white and African American students. It was soon rated one of the best schools in Chicago.

The South Side was traditionally an African American part of the city.

Michelle studied hard. She was surrounded by classmates who had all been selected to attend Whitney Young because they were among the smartest students in the city. Michelle's competitive streak meant that she wanted to make sure her grades were as good as those of her classmates. Even though she was a straight-A student, she still found time to learn the piano, take dance lessons, and be the treasurer of the student council. Her hard work paid off and she joined the National Honor Society. This was a club that helped to encourage the smartest students with the best grades around the country.

Michelle grew used to traveling to school by bus. She used the journey to read and study.

Michelle's close friends included Santita Jackson, daughter of civil rights leader Jesse Jackson.

OFF TO PRINCETON

Craig's basketball career and good grades earned him a place at the **Ivy League** Princeton University in New Jersey. The Robinsons were very proud of their son. Michelle figured that, if her brother could go to Princeton, so could she. Not everyone thought like her. A school counselor told her that Princeton was a step too far, and she should not aim so high.

Michelle was determined to follow in her brother's footsteps. In the summer of 1981, her dad drove her 12 hours to start her first semester at Princeton. She had accomplished her goal.

The name of Michelle's high school honored Whitney Young, a key leader of the struggle for black rights.

UNIVERSITY LIFE

Arriving at an Ivy League university in the 1980s was a strange experience for an African American student from the South Side of Chicago. Most of Michelle's fellow students were white and came from privileged backgrounds. Princeton's traditions did not really accommodate black students. The university was set up in such a way that it excluded African Americans from many aspects of college life. For example, Princeton's eating clubs held dinners and dances for students—but only white students were invited.

Princeton University was founded in 1746, making it one of the oldest academic institutions in America.

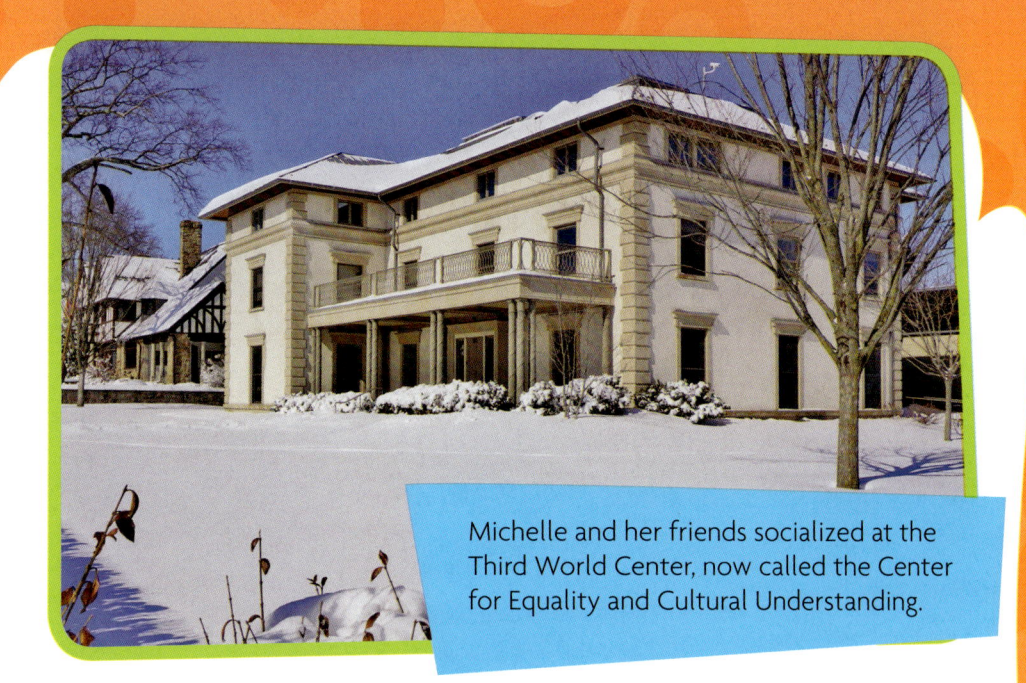

Michelle and her friends socialized at the Third World Center, now called the Center for Equality and Cultural Understanding.

HONOR STUDENT

Because they were excluded from these clubs, Michelle and her friends hung out at the Third World Center. The lack of **integration** between black and white students shocked Michelle. In her last year at Princeton, she wrote a paper about how it felt to be black at the college. It was highly critical of her experiences.

Despite the **prejudice** she had experienced at Princeton, Michelle worked hard and graduated with honors. Her grades were good enough for her to apply to law school. The toughest law school in the country to get into was Harvard—so that's where Michelle decided to go!

SLAVERY

When Michelle was 10, her grandparents moved from Chicago back to South Carolina, where her family had originated.

Michelle still had many relatives living in South Carolina. As she learned about the family's past, she discovered that her great-great-grandfather, Jim Robinson, had been a slave in the state. He had worked on a rice **plantation** called Friendfield, where he was one of around 500 slaves. Growing rice was hard work, so Southern plantations depended on slaves. Slavery was not outlawed until 1863.

Many generations of a family sometimes worked together as slaves.

FEATURE: SLAVERY

This wooden church still stands on the Friendfield plantation in South Carolina.

Slaves working on plantations growing cotton, tobacco, and rice had no rights. They were treated as the property of their white owners. They were not paid and they lived in cramped, basic conditions. Beatings were common, and many slaves died of mistreatment. Children born to slaves became slaves themselves.

After the Civil War (1861–1865), many slaves became **sharecroppers**. They farmed on poor land that could hardly support them. Their lives remained bitterly hard.

Sharecropper families had to borrow money to buy seeds, and often became trapped in debt.

Law and CIVIC DUTY

During her three years at Harvard Law School, Michelle volunteered to give legal advice to people who could not afford lawyers.

Each summer, Michelle returned to Chicago to work as an **intern** at the law firm Sidley Austin. The firm was impressed by Michelle. When she graduated Harvard in 1988, Sidley Austin offered her a full-time job. At the age of 24, Michelle was living back in her home town—and although in her twenties she was making more money than her dad!

After seven years away at Princeton and Harvard, Michelle was thrilled to be home again. Her new life in Chicago was very different from her old life in the city, however.

MEET THE GREATS: **MICHELLE OBAMA**

QUICK FACTS
- Michelle was a talented lawyer but she became unsatisfied by her job.
- Michelle was influenced by Barack to become more involved in social issues.

Michelle did not find it much fun to write contracts for Barney the dinosaur!

YOUNG WOMAN IN THE CITY

Michelle no longer had to ride the bus around the city. Now she not only earned enough money to buy a car, she could also afford to pay back her student loans and set up her own home. She did not break with her past entirely. She chose to move back to her old home on Euclid Avenue. She rented the apartment where she had been brought up from her parents. They moved downstairs, where they lived in the apartment that had belonged to Michelle's late aunt.

BECOMING A MENTOR

Michelle worked on the legal contracts for Barney, the purple dinosaur. Her colleagues thought she was lucky to have such a fun client, but Michelle was already thinking that **corporate** law was perhaps not for her. One of her other responsibilities at Sidley Austin was to **mentor** a summer intern. Like Michelle, the intern was a Harvard law student. The first thing she noticed about him was that he had an unusual name.

On his first day as an intern, Barack Obama was late. That did not impress Michelle, but everybody else in her firm thought Barack was great. They also thought that the two of them would make a good couple.

Barack Obama was 27 years old when Michelle met him.

This stone in Chicago marks the site of Michelle and Barack's first kiss.

Michelle was not interested in dating Barack. Her job was only to make sure he got a good feel for the firm. But she soon realized that Barack needed little guidance from her. He was three years older than her, and had more work experience than she had.

Barack asked Michelle on a date, but she resisted. Finally, she agreed to go to the movies. After that first date, they spent a lot of time together. One time, Barack took Michelle to a church where he was speaking in a community meeting.

Two things happened at the meeting. First, Michelle realized what a special man Barack was and that he genuinely wanted to help people. Second, it made her think about what she truly wanted to do. She decided that she wanted to use her legal training to help people.

A CHANGE IN DIRECTION

Over the summer of 1989, Barack and Michelle became a couple. At the end of the summer, however, Barack had to go back to Harvard to finish his remaining two years of law school. During that time, Michelle realized that she was deeply in love with Barack and wanted to plan a future with him.

Barack had grown up in Hawaii, but later considered Chicago his home.

Michelle decided that doing public service at City Hall would be more rewarding than working in law.

Around the same time, Michelle's best friend from Princeton, Suzanne Alele, died from cancer. The shock of losing Suzanne made Michelle look closely at her own life. Meanwhile, she was also influenced by watching Barack's commitment to helping the African American community and people who were less fortunate than himself.

Michelle did some thinking. She realized that she hated being a corporate lawyer, even though she was very good at the job. But she needed money because she had loans to pay. In addition, she knew how proud her parents were of everything she had achieved so far. She decided to stick with her job.

A NEW CAREER

Another tragedy finally led Michelle to change her mind. Fraser Robinson had always had poor health because of his multiple sclerosis. In late 1990, his health began to decline, and he died in March 1991, aged just 55. Her father's death left Michelle devastated but also aware that time was short. She finally decided that she had to change careers.

In 1991, Michelle quit her job and went to work for City Hall as an assistant to the mayor of Chicago. She worked with local communities on issues such as trash collection. It was a far cry from her high-powered legal life, but she was much happier! The following year, she married Barack in Chicago.

Michelle and Barack were married on October 3, 1992.

Social ACTIVISM

From early in her legal career, Michelle was unhappy working for big firms. She knew that she wanted a career that helped others.

She had wanted to be involved in helping others since her student days. While still at Princeton, she had set up an afterschool club for the children of African American professors. After she quit her law job back in Chicago, Michelle tried to make sure that the work she did added value to her community. She worked for Public Allies for three years after leaving the mayor's office. Her aim was to find young people who could help their own communities.

Public Allies aimed to give a voice to communities that had little representation in Chicago politics.

FEATURE: SOCIAL ACTIVISM

Michelle wanted to help tackle problems such as the poverty that existed alongside Chicago's wealth.

She looked for young people who were traditionally overlooked for such roles. She encouraged them to speak up for those whose voices were usually ignored.

After making Public Allies a success, Michelle worked a series of jobs based on helping the community. The jobs led her to the University of Chicago Medical Center, where her role was to **integrate** the hospital with the South Side neighborhood, which was mainly black. The job was perfect for her.

Many Chicagoans lived in run-down tenements and other poor quality housing.

25

A Political WIFE

In 2008, Michelle was busy. She had a demanding job at the University of Chicago Medical Center and two young daughters to care for.

She also had a husband who had decided to run for president of the United States. Michelle had first reluctantly agreed to let Barack run for public office back in 1996, when he wanted to be elected to the Illinois senate. She was happy to help collect signatures to get him on the ballot and to knock on doors to ask people to support her husband. Once Barack got elected to the state senate, however, the reality of being a political wife hit her. Her husband was away most of the week in the state capital, Springfield, while she continued to work in Chicago.

MEET THE GREATS: **MICHELLE OBAMA**

QUICK FACTS

- When Barack became a politician, Michelle was left to support the couple's family.
- Michelle helped Barack's campaign to run for president.

FAMILY LIFE

If it was tough being a political wife without children, it soon became a lot tougher. The Obamas's first daughter, Malia Ann, was born on July 4, 1998. Malia's sister, Natasha (Sasha) Marian, followed on June 10, 2001. With Barack away so much, Michelle hired a babysitter, and her mom helped her as much as she could. Michelle had told her employers at the medical center that she would only take the job if she had time to be a mom. The hospital had to allow her to attend school events and do tasks like taking her girls to the dentist. The hospital agreed because they knew how good Michelle would be at her job.

Barack spent the week working in the Illinois State Capitol in Springfield.

Michelle had to work harder at home to support Barack's rising political career.

NATIONAL OFFICE

In 2003, Barack decided he wanted to run for the U.S. Senate. Michelle was not sure that this was the best decision for the family. She realized it was the right move for Barack's political career. However, she also knew that if Barack became a senator, he would have to live in Washington, D.C.

Michelle loved family life in Chicago. She loved her job, and the family needed her salary. The girls were growing up and were very happy in the city. Michelle decided with Barack that, if he got elected, Michelle and the girls would stay behind in Chicago. Barack would head off to Washington, D.C., on his own.

Barack Obama addresses the Democratic National Convention in 2004. His success surprised everyone—but not his wife!

Michelle might have secretly hoped her husband did not win the seat for the sake of the family. However, she also knew how important it was for African Americans that he was elected. At the time, only four black senators had ever been elected to the U.S. Senate.

A BREAKTHROUGH CONVENTION

In July 2004, Barack was asked to give the **keynote speech** at the **convention** where the Democratic Party chose its candidate for the presidential election. Usually a member of Congress gave the speech, rather than a state senator like Barack. Michelle knew it was a great honor to be asked.

She also knew Barack's skill as a public speaker. She believed it was possible that the speech would change everything for him, for her, and for their family. And it did. The speech electrified not just the convention but the whole country. Soon people were talking about Barack Obama running for the presidency in 2008. He was not yet even a U.S. senator!

After all the favorable publicity, Barack was elected to the U.S. Senate with a huge majority. He spent his time in Washington, D.C. Michelle and the girls got used to his being away from home for even longer periods. With the help of her mom, babysitters, and her friends—and Barack, when he was around—Michelle somehow made everything work.

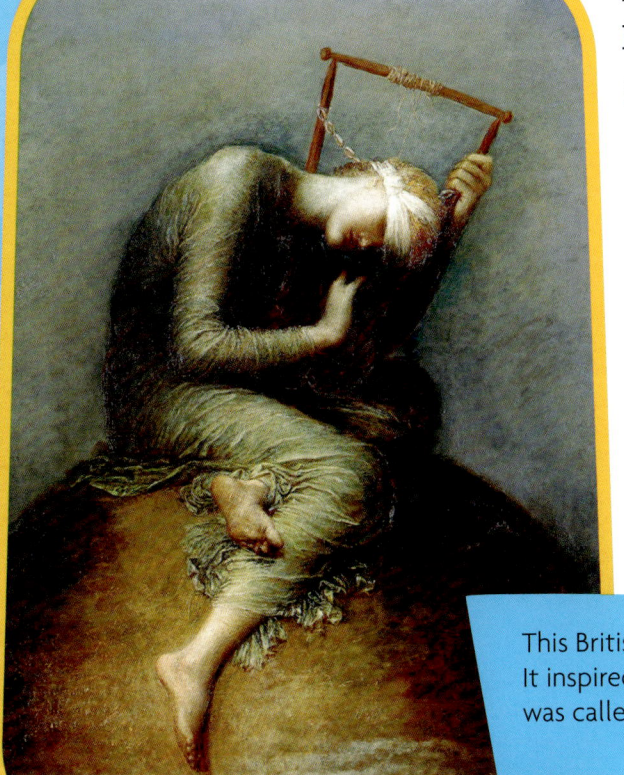

This British painting of 1886 is entitled *Hope*. It inspired Barack Obama's speech, which was called "The Audacity of Hope."

The speech at the Democratic Convention had another unexpected result. After Michelle married Barack, in 1992, he had written a book named *Dreams from My Father*. Now that Barack was famous, the book became a best seller. This meant the family no longer had to worry about money.

BECOMING THE FIRST LADY

When Barack decided that he would try to become U.S. president, Michelle joked that it would make life easier if he won. At least then the whole family would move to Washington, D.C. Michelle did not oppose her husband's decision to run. Instead, she asked him a lot of questions about how life would be if the family moved to the White House.

Michelle rides a bumper car while helping her husband campaign for the presidency.

Michelle and TV host Oprah Winfrey (center) watch Barack deliver a speech during his campaign.

Her questions were soon answered. Barack announced that he was running in February 2007. Michelle cut back on her job to help her husband. Like him, she toured the country meeting people and giving speeches. Her only rule was that she was never away from the girls for more than one night. Michelle was as popular as her husband! Everyone wanted to meet this **dynamic** young woman who was not only smart but glamorous.

In November 2008, Barack Obama was elected the 44th President of the United States and Michelle became First Lady. At the start of the new year, the family, plus their new puppy and Michelle's mother, all moved to the White House.

The First LADY

Michelle described the role of the First Lady as the only job where you can choose to focus on anything you want for the length of the presidency.

Michelle was the first African American First Lady and she followed in a long line of First Ladies who had used their position to try to do good just as Michelle had done in her working life. Being First Lady is, as Michelle pointed out, a job that is unpaid, a platform with no power, with staff but no budget.

Michelle and her daughters moved into the White House with President Obama.

FEATURE: THE FIRST LADY

First Lady Eleanor Roosevelt visits U.S. soldiers during World War II (1939–1945). She focused on improving the rights of African Americans and poor children.

First Ladies such as Eleanor Roosevelt and Betty Ford worked hard to improve life for Americans. Michelle launched four major initiatives while she was First Lady. The aim of Let's Move (2010) was to get young people fit. Joining Forces (2011) was an initiative to get Americans to support veterans. During Barack's second term, she launched the Reach Higher Initiative (2014) to keep children in higher education. The following year, Let Girls Learn worked to get girls around the world to attend school.

Michelle (in yellow) speaks at a children's sports event held by the U.S. Olympic Team in 2012.

The White House AND AFTER

Between 2008 and 2017, home for Michelle and her daughters, the descendants of slaves, was the White House in Washington, D.C.

While Barack ran the country as president and commander in chief, Michelle busied herself with working on causes she believed were important to the whole country. She wanted to draw attention to some of the major problems affecting the United States, such as the growing problem of **obesity** in young people. She also wanted to highlight the importance of the military in the nation's life and the lack of provision for girls' education around the world. But above all, she wanted to make sure that she continued to be mom-in-chief to her two girls!

MEET THE GREATS: MICHELLE OBAMA

QUICK FACTS
- Michelle tried to live as normally as possible in the White House.
- She launched a series of programs to help Americans.

Michelle supervises young people working on the vegetable patch.

When the Obamas moved to the White House, Malia and Sasha were ten and seven. Michelle was determined to make life as normal as possible. The girls had to make their own beds, and they could go find snacks in the kitchen just like at home.

WORKING TO IMPROVE AMERICA

One of the first things Michelle did was to plant a vegetable patch at the White House. She believed fresh food was important to health, and wanted to show how easy it was to grow fruit and vegetables.

What seemed a very simple idea took some persuading. Michelle was digging up National Park land! Eventually she got her way, and created a community garden that still exists today.

FASHION ICON

Michelle understood the importance of her appearance, and the impact her clothes could make. A white gown she wore to a ball where she danced with Barack made global headlines. As First Lady she helped to promote American designers by wearing their outfits. Although fashion was important, however, so was a bargain. Michelle was as happy to wear ready-made clothes as an expensive designer gown. She knew what a luxury it was to afford expensive clothes.

As First Lady, Michelle became well known for her sense of style and fashion.

LET'S MOVE

The White House garden was a success. The Obamas ate the vegetables they grew, and local kids helped plant and harvest the crops and ate some of the produce. Michelle wanted to take her healthy **crusade** further. Almost one-third of American children were overweight when Barack became president. In 2010, Michelle, who loved working out, launched Let's Move. The aim of the program was to get children exercising and to teach them about **nutrition** so they could make good food choices. Michelle believed this was the best start any child could make.

Michelle dances with talk show host Ellen DeGeneres to promote Let's Move.

This official portrait of Michelle and her family in the White House was taken in 2011.

MEETING FAMOUS PEOPLE

One of the many jobs of FLOTUS (First Lady of the United States) is accompanying the President when he meets other heads of state and royalty. Two of the most interesting people Michelle met during her time as First Lady were Queen Elizabeth II of the United Kingdom and Nelson Mandela, who was president of South Africa. Queen Elizabeth and Nelson Mandela had very different lives. Queen Elizabeth had been born into royalty and had been brought up surrounded by great privilege. Nelson Mandela had spent 27 years in jail for **terrorism** during his campaign to gain rights for black South Africans. However, both shared a belief in the importance of duty to one's country. Michelle identified with that duty.

A SECOND TERM

When Barack was reelected as president in 2012, Michelle knew what she wanted to work on: education. Education had gotten Michelle and Barack to the White House, and she believed that a good education was essential to create opportunity. She also knew that many millions of children are denied an education. Michelle started two initiatives. The Reach Higher program encouraged children from deprived and ethnic minority backgrounds to go to college. The Let Girls Learn program tried to help more than 98 million girls worldwide who are denied even a basic education.

Michelle gives a speech to support her husband's successful campaign for a second term.

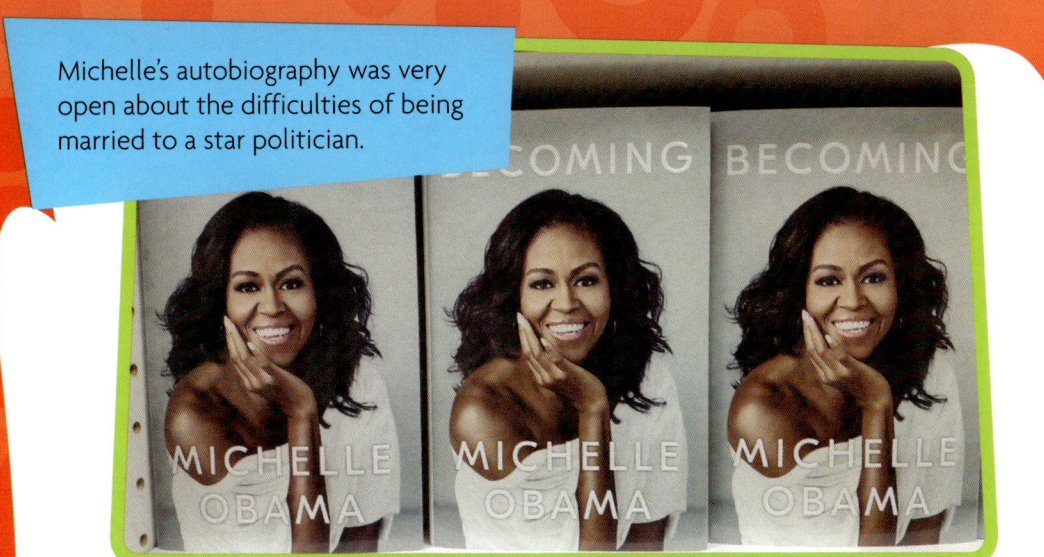

Michelle's autobiography was very open about the difficulties of being married to a star politician.

LIFE AFTER THE WHITE HOUSE

In January 2017, the Obamas left the White House after eight years. Michelle could make her own toast once again and load her own dishwasher, even if there were Secret Service agents in her yard. Such experiences were very enjoyable for Michelle, who had missed normal life.

Michelle continued with her programs to improve the life of Americans. She often worked on new initiatives with Barack. Like her husband, Michelle also became a successful writer. Her **autobiography**, *Becoming*, topped best-seller lists around the world. Her book tour was so successful that in 2019 she made another national tour. Michelle Obama had proved to the world yet again what a remarkable woman she had become.

Timeline

1964 • Born on January 17 in Chicago, Illinois, to Fraser and Marian Robinson.

1977 • Attends Whitney M. Young High School, Chicago's first magnet high school.

1981 • Goes to Princeton University, New Jersey.

1985 • Graduates from Princeton with honors and gets into Harvard Law School.

1988 • Graduates from Harvard, and is hired as an associate attorney at Sidley Austin law firm in Chicago.

1989 • Mentors an intern named Barack Obama in the summer, and later starts dating him.

1991 • Fraser Robinson dies, aged 55 years.

1992 • Michelle and Barack Obama marry on October 3 in Chicago.

1996 • Barack is elected to the Illinois State Senate. Michelle joins the University of Chicago, working in the Health Center.

1998 • The Obama's first daughter, Malia Ann, is born on July 4.

2001 • A second daughter, Natasha (Sasha) Marian, is born on June 10.

2008 • Michelle becomes the first African American First Lady after Barack Obama is elected the 44th president of the United States.

2009 • The Obamas move into the White House on January 20. Michelle plants a vegetable patch in the White House garden.

2010 • Michelle starts the Let's Move program to get young people to exercise more.

2011 • Michelle's next initiative, launched with Dr. Jill Biden, wife of Vice President Joe Biden, is to help service people, veterans, and their families.

2012 • Barack is elected for a second term. Michelle speaks at the Democratic Convention in Charlotte, North Carolina.

2014 • Michelle launches the Reach Higher initiative to encourage more young people to go to college.

2015 • She launches Let Girls Learn, a program to help girls around the world go to school.

• Michelle and her family join a march in Selma, Alabama, to celebrate the 50th anniversary of the civil rights movement.

2017 • The Obamas leave the White House.

2018 • Michelle publishes *Becoming*, her number-one best-selling autobiography, and undertakes a tour to promote the book.

2019 • The success of the book leads to an international book tour.

KEY INITIATIVES
- Let's Move (2010)
- Join Forces (2011)
- Reach Higher (2014)
- Let Girls Learn (2015)

Glossary

autobiography A written account of someone's own life.

civil rights People's right to social and political freedom.

commute A daily journey to and from school or work.

convention A large meeting of people to achieve a task.

corporate Related to large firms, or corporations.

crusade A campaign that aims to change something for the better.

dynamic Full of energy.

integrate To bring different groups of people equally into a group or institution.

integration The quality of being integrated.

intern A student who undertakes a job, often without pay, to gain work experience.

Ivy League A group of long-established U.S. universities with high academic status.

keynote speech A speech that outlines the key issues facing a conference.

magnet school A school designed to attract smart students from a wide area.

mentor An experienced advisor who helps a younger or less experienced colleague.

multiple sclerosis A serious disease that affects the spine and the brain.

nutrition Healthy eating.

obesity The state of being very overweight.

plantation A large estate or farm used to grow crops.

prejudice Hostility toward someone based on their race, sex, or other factors.

progressive Wanting to change society through reform.

sharecroppers Farmers who give their suppliers part of their crop to pay for seeds and farming equipment.

terrorism Using violence to try to achieve political aims.

Further Resources

Books

Endsley, Kezia. *Michelle Obama: 44th First Lady and Health and Education Advocate.* Leading Women. New York: Cavendish Square, 2014.

Machajewski, Sarah. *Michelle Obama.* Superwomen Role Models. New York: PowerKids Press, 2016.

Obama, Michelle. *Becoming.* New York: Crown, 2018.

Stine, Megan. *Who Is Michelle Obama?* Who Is? New York: Grosset and Dunlap, 2013.

Websites

History.com
www.history.com/topics/first-ladies/michelle-obama
A biography of Michelle and her achievements as First Lady.

Michelle Obama
www.biography.com/people/michelle-obama-307592
A biography and video about Michelle Obama's time as First Lady.

Obama Foundation
www.obama.org/our-story
A detailed timeline of Barack and Michelle's lives and achievements from the Obama Foundation.

Reach Higher
www.bettermakeroom.org/reach-higher/
Michelle's program to encourage all students to get the best education they can.

Publisher's note to educators and parents: Our editors have carefully reviewed these websites to ensure that they are suitable for students. Many websites change frequently, however, and we cannot guarantee that a site's future contents will continue to meet our high standards of quality and educational value. Be advised that students should be closely supervised whenever they access the Internet.

Index

A
African Americans 12, 13, 22, 24, 30, 34
Alele, Suzanne 22

B
Barney the dinosaur 18, 19
Becoming 43
Bryn Mawr Public Elementary School 8

C
campaign, Barack Obama's election 32, 33, 42
Chicago 4, 6, 8, 9, 12, 16, 21, 22, 23, 29
City Hall, Chicago 22, 23
corporate law 16, 18, 19, 22

D
Democratic Convention 32
Democratic National Convention 30
Democratic Party 30
Dreams from My Father 32

E
education, policy 42
Elizabeth II, Queen 41

F
fashion 39
First Lady 4, 34, 35, 39, 41
Ford, Betty 35
Friendfield 14, 15

H
Harvard Law School 4, 13, 16, 21
health 36, 40

I
integration 13, 25
Ivy League 11, 12

J
Jackson, Santita 11
Joining Forces 35

L
legal career 16, 18, 19
Let Girls Learn 35, 42
Let's Move 35, 40

M
magnet schools 8, 9, 10
Mandela, Nelson 41
marriage 23
mutiple sclerosis 6, 23

N
National Honor Society 10
nutrition 38, 40

O
Obama, Barack 4, 19, 20, 21, 22, 23, 26, 28, 29, 30, 31, 32, 33, 36, 42
Obama, family 41
Obama, Malia 28, 38
Obama, Natasha 28, 38
obesity 36, 40

P R
Princeton University 11, 12, 13, 24
Public Allies 24, 25
Reach Higher 35, 42
Robinson, Craig 6, 8, 11
Robinson, Fraser 6, 23
Robinson, Marian 6
Roosevelt, Eleanor 35

S
Senate, Illinois 26
Senate, U.S. 29, 30, 31
sharecroppers 15
Sidley Austin 16, 19
slavery 4, 14–15
social activism 24–25
South Carolina 14
South Side 6, 8, 9, 12
Springfield 26, 28

T U V
Third World Center 13
University of Chicago Medical Center 25, 26, 28
vegetable patch, White House 38, 39, 40

W Y
Washington, DC 29, 31, 32
White House 32, 33, 34, 36, 38, 43
Whitney M. Young Magnet High School 9, 10
Winfrey, Oprah 33
Young, Whitney 11